Where Are the Great Pyramids?

by Dorothy and Thomas Hoobler

illustrated by Jerry Hoare

Grosset & Dunlap
An Imprint of Penguin Random House

To our daughter Ellen and
our son-in-law Mandar—DH & TH

GROSSET & DUNLAP
Penguin Young Readers Group
An Imprint of Penguin Random House LLC

Text copyright © 2015 by Dorothy Hoobler and Thomas Hoobler.
Illustrations copyright © 2015 by Penguin Random House LLC. All rights reserved.
Published by Grosset & Dunlap, an imprint of Penguin Random House LLC,
345 Hudson Street, New York, New York 10014. GROSSET & DUNLAP
is a trademark of Penguin Random House LLC. Printed in the USA.

Library of Congress Cataloging-in-Publication Data is available.

ISBN 978-0-448-48409-9   10 9 8 7 6 5 4 3 2 1

CONTENTS

Where Are the Great Pyramids?

The Great Pyramids of Egypt are the most famous buildings in the world. They stand outside Cairo, the capital and biggest city in Egypt. Almost everybody has seen a picture of them. They are also among the world's largest buildings, the oldest buildings still standing, and the most closely studied buildings. In ancient times, they were one of the Seven Wonders of the World.

The Seven Wonders of the Ancient World

Greek tourists of the first and second centuries BC could buy guidebooks that listed spectacular places to visit. Seven of these became known as the Seven Wonders of the World. Besides the Great Pyramids, they are:

1) *The Hanging Gardens of Babylon*. The king of the Babylonian Empire married a woman from a land where many trees and plants grew. She became homesick. To please her, the king had fabulous gardens built on terraces.

2) *The Temple of Artemis at Ephesus*. The king of Lydia, known for his great wealth, had a beautiful temple built at Ephesus, a city in modern-day Turkey.

3) *The Statue of Zeus at Olympia*. This gigantic statue was covered with ivory, gold, and precious stones.

4) *The Mausoleum at Halicarnassus*. Mausolus, a

wealthy governor in the Persian Empire, ordered a fabulous tomb built for himself and his wife. Today, the word *mausoleum* is used to mean any large tomb.

5) *The Colossus of Rhodes.* To celebrate winning a war, the people of Rhodes built an enormous statue of the sun god Helios in their harbor.

6) *The Lighthouse of Alexandria.* The successor to Alexander the Great built a huge lighthouse in the harbor of this Egyptian city to guide ships in the Mediterranean.

The Colossus of Rhodes

Today, all of those wonders have disappeared—except the pyramids.

The pyramids were not built for people to live in. They were tombs for the pharaohs, the rulers of Egypt. Pharaohs were the link between the Egyptian people and their gods. In fact, the pharaohs themselves were regarded as gods. Whatever the pharaohs wished people to do, it was done. Thus, when pharaohs commanded thousands of people to work for many years to build their tombs, they did it.

There are more than one hundred pyramids still standing in Egypt. But many of them are little more than heaps of rubble. The three largest are known as the Great Pyramids. The oldest of the three was built about 4,500 years ago.

The ancient Egyptians believed the pharaoh would live in another world after death. That's why it was important to preserve his body and place it somewhere safe—like inside a pyramid.

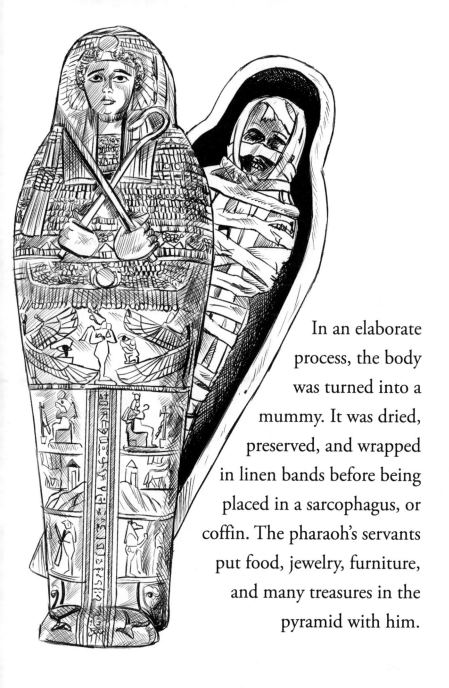

In an elaborate process, the body was turned into a mummy. It was dried, preserved, and wrapped in linen bands before being placed in a sarcophagus, or coffin. The pharaoh's servants put food, jewelry, furniture, and many treasures in the pyramid with him.

The pharaohs wanted to make sure their tombs were not disturbed. So the pyramid builders carefully hid the passages that led to the pharaoh's burial chamber. They set traps for anyone who tried to break in. Even so, tomb robbers managed to get inside and steal treasures.

Over the centuries, Egypt declined. But the Great Pyramids remained. When later visitors arrived, they were astonished by what they saw. No one had seen anything like the pyramids. A Greek known as Herodotus arrived in Egypt in the fifth century BC. The pyramids were already thousands of years old then. Like so many others, he asked, "Who could have built these pyramids? How did they do it?"

Today, scientists still seeking the answers to such questions. We know more about Egypt than Herodotus did, yet unsolved mysteries remain. Today's scientists are making new discoveries, but the pyramids still hold many secrets.

Herodotus

The Greek historian Herodotus was born around 480 BC. He was the first European traveler to visit and write about Egypt. He called its wonders "more in number than any other land." Herodotus described the process of mummification (preserving bodies), which was still being done when he visited. He also described how the pyramids were built, but modern scientists think some of what he wrote isn't true. It had been a very long time since anyone had actually built one.

He was most accurate when he wrote about the life of the Egyptian people. He was shocked at how different they were from the Greeks. "The Egyptians appear to have reversed the ordinary practices of mankind," he wrote. "Women attend markets and are employed in trade, while men stay at home and do the weaving! Men in Egypt carry loads on their heads, women on their shoulders. Women pass water standing up, men sitting down."

Herodotus wrote everything he could find out about the history of the countries he passed through. Today he is known as "the Father of History."

CHAPTER 1
The Gift of the Nile

It took a rich and powerful country to build the Great Pyramids. Egypt was rich because of its location along the Nile River. Herodotus called Egypt "the gift of the Nile," and he was right.

The Nile's greatest gift was the dark, fertile soil it brought to Egypt every year when it flooded. In some countries, farmers are afraid of floods. But in Egypt, the flood left behind a new covering of fresh soil. The soil deposited by the Nile was called *kemet*—the black land. The *kemet* was only about thirteen miles wide. Beyond that on both sides, was *deshret*—the red land, which was desert. Nearly all Egyptians lived in the black land, growing wheat and barley. These grains were stored for use all year round.

The red land was a barrier that protected Egypt from outside invaders. In the north, the Nile divides into many branches, so the land is swampy. Enemies could not cross that land either, so Egypt was safe from foreign conquerors for many centuries.

Without the Nile, workers could not have brought massive stones to the building sites of the pyramids. Roads built on sand could not carry such heavy loads, but boats and rafts could.

Egypt also had a strong government with one person at the top—the pharaoh. This kind of government was necessary to carry out such immense projects as building a pyramid. Originally, there were two communities along the Nile. One, called Upper Egypt, was in the south. That sounds confusing, because on our maps, south is always on the lower part of the map. But the Nile flows from south to north, so Upper Egypt was upstream. The other community was farther down the Nile, near the place where the river divides into many branches. That was Lower Egypt.

Around 3100 BC, a ruler of Upper Egypt named Narmer conquered Lower Egypt and unified the country. He built a new capital at the midpoint between the two Egypts. The city was

Mediterranean Sea

LOWER
EGYPT

Memphis

UPPER
EGYPT

Nile River

Red Sea

known as Memphis, and about thirty thousand people lived there. No other city in the world was that large.

The title for Egypt's ruler was *pharaoh*, which means "great house." At his coronation, he was named king of Upper and Lower Egypt. A double crown was placed on his head. At his death, a son or other family member took his place. It was the pharaoh's duty to keep Egypt prosperous. He guarded Egypt even after his death. That was why the Egyptians went to such great lengths to preserve his body.

The pharaohs were at the top of a society shaped like a pyramid. Below them were the royal family and officials. Then came wealthy landowners, scribes, craftsmen, artists, farmers, and slaves. Scribes were important because they learned the complicated Egyptian writing, called hieroglyphs. The largest number of people were peasants who grew food and also worked on the pyramids. Because the farms were so fertile, many workers could spend their time pyramid building.

The Gods of Egypt

The Egyptians had many gods. They are often shown as having human bodies and animal heads. The animal head showed the quality of that particular god. One of the most important was Horus, the falcon god. (The falcon flew higher than any other creature, watching over all.) His image appears next to the name of the pharaoh in Egyptian writing.

CHAPTER 2
From Mud to Stone

The history of Egypt is divided into dynasties, the times when a particular family ruled the country. In all, there were thirty-one dynasties, divided into three groups, called the Old Kingdom, the Middle Kingdom, and the New Kingdom.

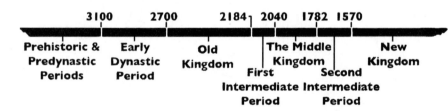

3100	2700	2184	2040	1782	1570
Prehistoric & Predynastic Periods	Early Dynastic Period	Old Kingdom	The Middle Kingdom		New Kingdom
			First Intermediate Period	Second Intermediate Period	

From the very first dynasty, the pharaohs were concerned with their tombs. In the beginning, pharaohs were buried in a place called Abydos, west of the Nile. The tombs were underground chambers carved from rock. Over time, the tombs became larger and grander. They were lined with bricks made from mud, and surrounded by smaller tombs. These may have contained the bodies of servants who had been sacrificed to serve their ruler in the afterlife.

The royal tombs began to be topped with mud brick buildings called *mastabas*. These were platforms with sloping sides. They were about thirty feet high, and had doorways that led to the burial chamber. Secret chambers held burial goods.

One of the largest of these early tombs held the body of a woman named Merneith. She was the wife of the pharaoh named Djet. When Djet died, their son Den was too young to rule. So Merneith carried out his duties. Some scientists think she was a pharaoh. Her tomb is located close to the tombs of male pharaohs. If Merneith was a pharaoh, she would be the world's earliest known female ruler.

The first pharaoh of the third dynasty was named Djoser. He appointed many skilled people to important posts. One was a scholar named

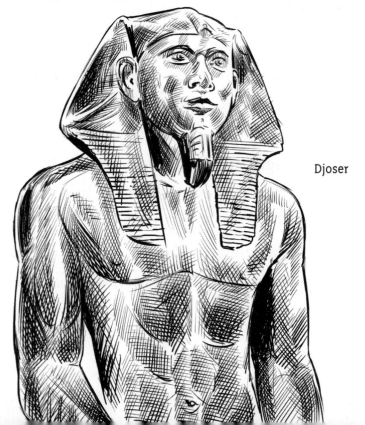

Djoser

Imhotep. He designed a new kind of tomb that would show Djoser's power. It began with a *mastaba* made of stone, not mud brick. On top of that was a second, smaller *mastaba*. Four more *mastabas* followed, each one smaller than the previous one.

The result was the Step Pyramid.

Located in Saqqara, across the Nile from Memphis, the Step Pyramid can still be seen today. It was the first large building made from stone. Like all the pyramids, it was west of the Nile. That was the direction of the setting sun, where ancient Egyptians believed the afterlife was.

And it was built to last. In 1924, an archeologist named Cecil Firth was exploring the inside of the Step Pyramid. He discovered a sealed room with no door but two small holes at eye level. When Firth looked inside, he found himself staring at a seated statue of the pharaoh Djoser. He was wearing a striped headdress. The eye sockets of the statue had originally been filled with crystal balls. Though they were empty now, Firth was staring into the face of a man who had lived 4,500 years ago.

Cecil Firth

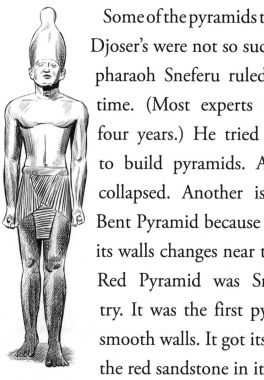

Some of the pyramids that followed Djoser's were not so successful. The pharaoh Sneferu ruled for a long time. (Most experts say twenty-four years.) He tried three times to build pyramids. At least one collapsed. Another is called the Bent Pyramid because the angle of its walls changes near the top. The Red Pyramid was Sneferu's last try. It was the first pyramid with smooth walls. It got its name from the red sandstone in its core.

Bent Pyramid

Originally white limestone covered the red sandstone core, making the sides smooth. But most of the limestone was later removed for other building projects. The Red Pyramid is popular with tourists today, because people can walk through its many corridors. Some scientists think Sneferu's burial chamber, somewhere inside, has yet to be discovered.

CHAPTER 3
The Great Pyramids of Giza

Khufu was the pharaoh who followed Sneferu. He created the first of the three Great Pyramids of Giza. These are the ones most often seen in photographs of Egypt. They are among the greatest construction projects in all of history. They were the mammoth tombs of Khufu and the pharaohs who came after him—Khafre and Menkaure. All three were built during the fourth dynasty (2613–2494 BC). They are located on the Giza Plateau, just outside modern Cairo.

Khufu

Khafre

Menkaure

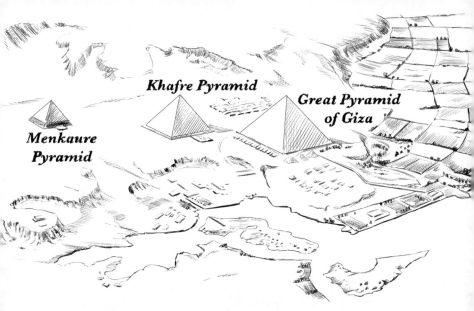

Khafre Pyramid

Great Pyramid
of Giza

Menkaure
Pyramid

The Great Pyramids were originally even more
spectacular than they are now. They were covered
with smooth white limestone.
At the top of each was a
pyramid-shaped cap, called a
pyramidion. It was covered
with gold. Scientists think the
pyramid shape was designed to
resemble the rays of the sun. Ra,
the sun god, was the chief god of
the Egyptians.

The core of each pyramid was granite and sandstone that came from far to the south, around Aswan. Most of the white limestone was later stripped off and used for other buildings. So the core is the part that we see today.

The pyramids did not stand alone. They

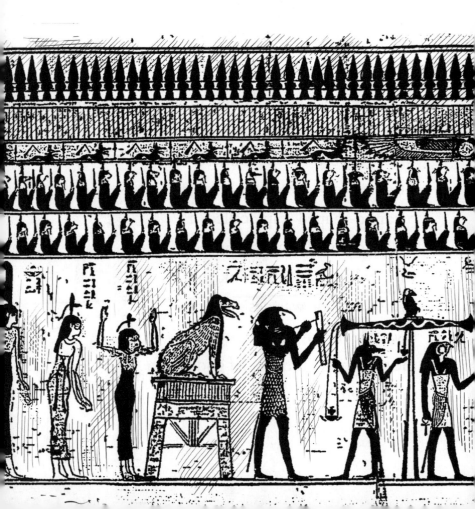

were part of a group of buildings that included a temple. Here, offerings of food and drink were presented daily for the dead pharaoh. Egyptians believed his needs in death were the same as in life. Smaller pyramids and *mastabas* were created nearby for royal relatives and high officials.

The Pyramid of Khufu (also called Cheops) is 481 feet high. It was the largest stone building on earth and remained the tallest for almost four thousand years. Khufu had a large family, and he put his nephew Hemiunu in charge of building his pyramid. Hemiunu's tomb is near Khufu's pyramid.

The granite for building Khufu's pyramid needed to be brought from hundreds of miles away. The only way to transport it was along the Nile in strong boats. But Egypt didn't have many trees for building boats. So Khufu sent people to the city of Byblos, in today's Lebanon. The Egyptians were able to buy strong cedar trees there. They built ships with the cedar. Two of the ships were buried near Khufu's pyramid.

The second Great Pyramid was intended for Khafre, Khufu's son. Herodotus says that Khafre was a cruel ruler. Khafre wanted his pyramid to be larger than his father's. Although the

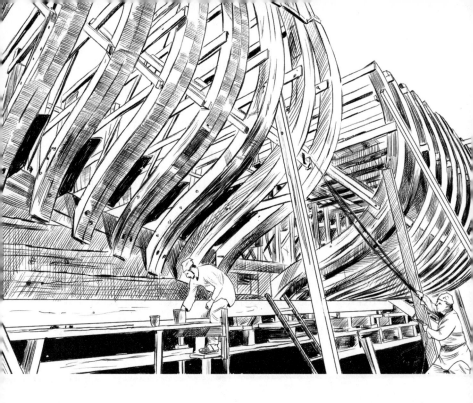

actual pyramid is only 448 feet tall, it rests on a higher part of the bedrock, and so appears taller. Its pyramidion is still in place. The other two pyramids originally had one, too, but they were removed for their gold.

The third pyramid was built by Menkaure, grandson of Khufu. His pyramid is the smallest of the group—originally 218 feet high.

Menkaure was remembered as one of the kindest rulers in Egypt's history. Perhaps this is because he didn't make people work so hard building his pyramid. He is also known for his wise judgments in disputes that were brought to him.

It may be hard to believe, but in the twelfth century AD, a ruler wanted to tear down the Great Pyramids. Kurds had conquered the country, and their ruler wanted to do away with these signs of

Egypt's power. He sent a large number of workers, who started with Menkaure's pyramid. They were only able to remove one or two stones each day. They had to split each stone into several pieces so that carts could carry them away. Finally, after eight months, the ruler decided the workers were wasting their time. But a large gash on the side of Menkaure's pyramid shows the damage they did.

Guarding the plateau of Giza is the largest statue in the world. With the body of a lion and

the face of a man, it is known as the Sphinx. (The face is said to be that of Khafre.) Between the Sphinx's paws is a *stela* or stone slab put up by a later pharaoh. The *stela* says that the pharaoh

had been hunting in Giza and fell asleep. A god came to him in a dream and commanded him to clear the sand that had covered the Sphinx. Many other, smaller sphinx statues have been built since.

Tallest Buildings

Khufu's pyramid was the tallest building in the world until AD 1311. In that year, a 525-foot tower was built for Lincoln Cathedral in England. A storm in 1549 blew down that tower, and Khufu's pyramid was again the tallest structure for another 340 years. Then, in 1889, the Eiffel Tower was completed in Paris. It was 1,063 feet tall—about as high as an eighty-story building.

The fourth dynasty was the high point of Egyptian pyramid building. Pyramids built later were much smaller. During the fifth and sixth dynasties, the annual floods were weaker. Crops failed. Famines resulted, and there weren't as many workers available for pyramid building. Throughout the centuries, Egypt went through times of greatness and times of trouble. Many different countries invaded. Through it all, the Great Pyramids have endured.

"The Father of Pots"

William Flinders Petrie was born in London in 1853. Even as a boy, he loved to measure things. Later he read a book that said the measurements of the pyramids contained the roots of all mathematics. So he went to Egypt to see for himself. After two years of work, he announced that all the measurements in the book were wrong.

More important, he started to collect examples of Egyptian pottery—even broken pieces. Petrie realized that pottery styles change over time. Linking the pottery to objects nearby could tell how old the objects were. His Egyptian guides gave him the name Abu Bagousheh, which means "the father of pots."

One of Petrie's greatest discoveries came in 1903, at Abydos. A worker found a small headless statue. Petrie saw a pharaoh's name on the bottom, and stopped all other work. The ground near the statue was carefully dug up and put through a sieve. At last the statue's head was found. It turned out to be the only known image of Khufu, the pharaoh who built the Great Pyramid.

CHAPTER 4
Building the Pyramids

How was it possible for the Egyptians to build the immense pyramids? Khufu's pyramid alone consists of 2.3 million stone blocks. The average one weighs 2.5 tons—about as much as a small pickup truck. But some stones used for the pharaoh's burial chamber weigh as much as eighty tons! A modern eighteen-wheeler truck can only carry a load about one-fourth that heavy—and the Egyptians moved these stones with human power alone.

How did they do it? The honest answer is, nobody really knows. But scientists have made some guesses. Workers must have cut the stones from quarries on the opposite side of the Nile, or farther away at Aswan in the south. The workers

probably used copper chisels, although none have been found in the quarries. So another way of splitting the stones has been suggested. This was to drive pieces of wood into cracks in the stone. Then water was poured into the cracks. When the wood swelled up, the stone would break.

Each pharaoh probably chose the spot for his own pyramid. The ground had to be smoothed and leveled. A pyramid rests on a square base, and has four sides. Each corner points to a direction of the compass.

The most amazing thing about the pyramids was moving the huge stones. First, they had to be brought down the Nile on wooden boats, made from the cedar that came from Lebanon.

From the river, they were moved to the building area. There were several ways this might have been done. One suggestion is that a canal was built from the Nile. Another idea is that workers built a causeway, or stone road, that led to the pyramid area. The huge stones had to be dragged along this road on sleds. (A wheeled cart holding something that heavy would be crushed.) A picture on a tomb wall showed men using ropes to drag a wooden sled that held such a stone. Recently, scientists have suggested a special method of dragging the stones across the soft sand.

Once the stones reached the building site, a new problem arose: how to move them up the side of the pyramid. Using ramps made of stone or wood seems like the only possible answer. A modern engineering company showed that 2½-ton concrete blocks could be dragged up a ramp by eighteen men at a rate of about twenty yards per minute.

That raises two other questions: how long would the job take, and how many workers would be needed? The ancient Greek historian Herodotus thought thousands of slaves built the pyramids. But modern scientists doubt that slaves were used. They have found the remains of workers' settlements.

There were houses with clothing for both men and women, and even children's toys. That meant the workers lived with their families. Evidence also shows that they ate bread, onions, and garlic, and drank beer three times a day. At the end of the nine-day Egyptian week, they had a feast of grilled fish or fowl, along with wine. This was better food than slaves would have had.

Notre-Dame
Cathedral

There was a workforce that labored on the pyramids all year round. During flooding season, these workers were helped by farmers who had spare time. In return, the farmers probably had their taxes lowered.

Scientists use different computer models to figure out how many workers were needed. For the Great Pyramid of Khufu, the best guess is between fifteen thousand and thirty thousand workers over a period of at least ten years. The pyramid had to be finished before the pharaoh died. (By comparison, Notre-Dame Cathedral in Paris took almost two hundred years to build, from AD 1163 to 1345.)

The workers were divided into gangs of two hundred men. Then each gang was split into teams of twenty. Some were so proud of their work that they left the name of their group on the walls inside the pyramid. Some names were: "Victorious Gang," "Enduring Gang," and even "Drunk Gang." One crew wrote "Friends of Khufu."

In a sense, each pyramid was built from the inside out. Food, clothing, and treasures that the king would need in the afterlife were placed in the burial chamber while it was still open to the outside. Then the rest of the pyramid was built around it. Narrow corridors were made to connect the chamber to the outside world.

The Egyptians were well aware that robbers often stole the treasures from tombs. So workers built false chambers and long corridors that led nowhere. It was dangerous to enter a maze if you did not know the correct way in—and out.

Tomb Robbers

Khafre's pyramid was the only one of the three Great Pyramids to remain sealed until modern times. In 1818, an Italian collector named Giovanni Belzoni discovered a small entrance. Though it was only four feet high and three and a half feet wide, he squeezed through. This was not easy, as Belzoni was six feet, six inches tall. But inside the burial chamber he found nothing but an empty sarcophagus with a broken lid on the floor. Ancient tomb robbers had been there before him.

Nearly all the pyramids and most of the stone tombs were looted for their treasure. Tomb robbing was a risky business. Traps had been set by the pyramid builders to capture the robbers. But scientists have learned that some of the tomb robbers had earlier worked to build the pyramids. So they knew how to avoid the traps.

CHAPTER 5
Living Forever

Since the pharaoh himself was a god, it was expected that he would go from this life to another when he died. He would live with the gods. The pyramid was a place where the pharaoh's body could be protected.

Eternal life began with a journey through the underworld. The *ka*, or life force, left the body at death, and then after burial, the *ba*, or soul, followed. Horus guided the dead to the hall

Anubis

of judgment. Waiting there was the god Anubis. Anubis had the head of a jackal. (The jackal was known for digging up graves and eating the dead.) He weighed the dead person's heart on a scale, against a feather. Osiris, ruler of the underworld, stood by watching, along with other gods. If the heart was too heavy, then a monster who was part hippo, part lion, and part crocodile ate it. No happy afterlife.

Osiris

Ammut

55

But if the feather balanced the heart, then the *ba* and the *ka* united to form the *akh*. The *akh* needed a body to reenter and make it live again. All the pleasures of earthly life would continue. To prepare the body for this happy existence, Egyptians developed methods to preserve the body after death. This is what is known as mummification.

When the pharaoh died, his body was brought by boat to the temple near his pyramid.

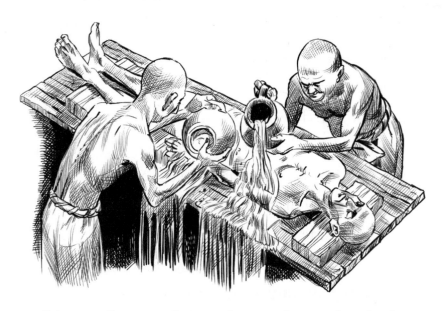

Mummification began by washing the body. This was not just to clean it. Water was thought to make the body pure and ready for rebirth. The next step was to remove the inner organs, which decayed quickly. Embalmers took out the brain by inserting hook-shaped tools through the nostrils. The skull was then packed with linen, also through the nostrils.

After that, embalmers cut open the abdomen and removed the stomach, intestines, lungs, and liver. The brain was thrown away. It was not considered important. The other organs were placed in natron, a kind of salt. The natron would dry them out. The organs were then put in special jars, and placed with the body in the tomb. The heart was left inside the body, for Egyptians believed it contained a person's intelligence and memory. It had to remain under the person's direct control.

The longest step in the process was to dry the entire body in the natron. Sometimes bags of natron were placed inside the stomach cavity as well. To fully dry a body took about forty days. Because the fingernails and toenails would fall off during this process, they were tied on with thread.

Drying made the body shrink. So embalmers filled it with linen and sawdust. That way the body looked more natural. The skin was softened with sweet-smelling oils. These oils also prevented bacteria from decaying the body.

Just as modern embalmers do, the Egyptians applied cosmetics to the dead. The hair was combed or styled. Some mummies have been found with hair extensions or wigs. The eye sockets were filled with fake eyes, and features like eyebrows were painted on.

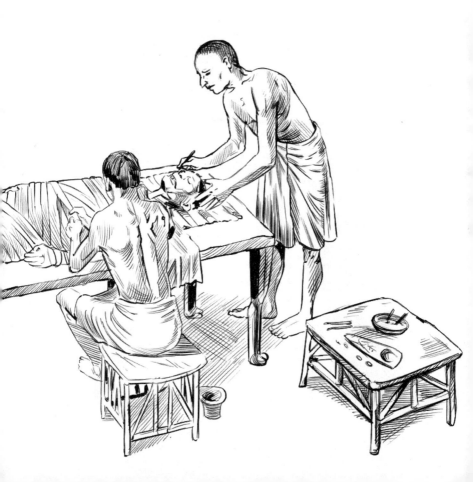

Egyptian Beauty Tips

Both men and women used cosmetics in Ancient Egypt. Black eyeliner was made from kohl, a soft mineral that was easily ground into powder. Green eyeliner was made from another mineral, malachite.

These materials were ground on a flat, triangular piece of stone called a palette.

Egyptians believed these eyeliners protected the eye from diseases. Modern scientists say there is some truth to this. Eyeliner probably shielded the eyes from the glare of the sun. Henna, a reddish-brown plant, was used to color fingernails and dye hair. It is still used today as a hair dye. Red ochre was mixed with fat to make lip gloss. Powdered ochre was also used as rouge. The ochre came from reddish clay that was dried and then pounded into powder.

Egyptians removed most of their body hair. Both men and women used razors, and also waxed their skin. One formula for the skin wax consisted of the crushed bones of a bird, fly dung, oil, sycamore juice, and cucumber.

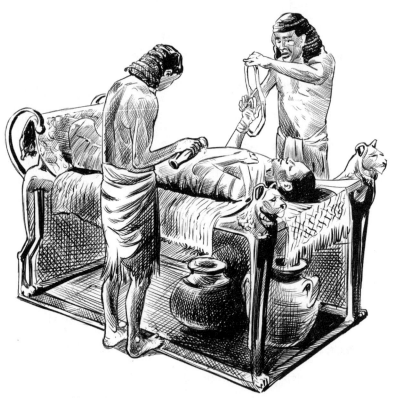

Finally, the body was wrapped in linen bands. Each arm and leg was separately wrapped before the embalmers covered the entire body. Priests said prayers at each step of the wrapping process. Sometimes religious charms were placed inside the linen bands. They were supposed to ward off evil spirits.

The priest who did the mummifying wore a mask with the head of a jackal. It made him look like the god Anubis. At the end of the process, the priest used a special tool to cut open the wrappings over the mouth of the mummy. This would allow the dead person to speak.

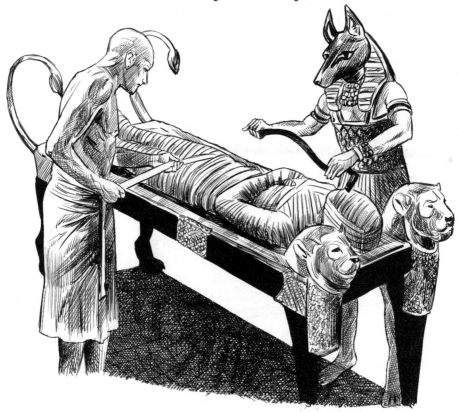

Afterward, the mummy was placed inside a coffin, which was usually made of wood. An image of the pharaoh's face and body was painted on the coffin. A funeral procession would follow it along the stone causeway to the tomb. There, while priests chanted spells and prayers, the coffin was stood upright. A high priest touched the eyes, nose, lips, ears, hands, and feet on the coffin. This was to "open" them for the afterlife.

Then the coffin was carried into the tomb until it reached the burial chamber. It was put inside a

sarcophagus. This was a larger chest, usually made
of stone, in the shape of a body. An image of the
dead pharaoh's face was on the sarcophagus. These
images were often covered with gold, because gold
was believed to be the flesh of the gods. Now the
pharaoh was ready for his journey to the afterlife,
the land of the gods.

Animal Mummies

Many mummies of animals have been found in Egyptian tombs. They were preserved with the same methods used on humans. Just as you might want to take a favorite pet with you when you died, so did the Egyptians. Among the most popular pets were cats, which sometimes are found in cat-shaped coffins, with painted faces. Dog mummies have also been discovered.

Larger animals, such as donkeys, gazelles, and lions, were also made into mummies. Because the process was expensive, they were usually buried only in royal tombs. A baboon mummy was found with its canine (pointed) teeth removed, so it would not be able to bite its owner.

Some creatures were made into mummies for religious reasons. People paid for them to be offered at temples during festivals. Crocodiles were sacred animals. Each year, they were said to lay their eggs just above where the Nile would flood. Thus, they were thought to be able to foretell the future. One crocodile mummy was discovered with baby crocodile mummies inside its mouth.

CHAPTER 6
Building for the Ages

Around 2375 BC, one of the last pyramids of the Old Kingdom era was built. It was intended for the pharaoh Unas. It was unusual because for the first time, the walls inside were covered with hieroglyphs. This writing was for a number of spells, or prayers. They were intended to help the dead person find his way through the underworld. Modern scientists called them pyramid texts. Centuries after Unas's time, such spells were written on scrolls that ordinary people could buy. Like the pharaohs, those who purchased them wanted to live forever, too. Collections of these spells are called *The Book of the Dead*.

About a century after Unas's time, the pyramid building stopped. Probably a series of droughts kept the annual floods from occurring. More people had to work on farms just to survive. Around 2100 BC, the pharaohs lost their power for a time, until another powerful family united the country again. The era known as the Middle Kingdom began.

The new pharaohs tried to continue the old ways. They even built a few new pyramids. But the new tombs were not as large and grand as the Old Kingdom ones. They were built of mud brick, which didn't last as well as the earlier pyramids. Today, the Middle Kingdom pyramids look like heaps of rubble. The last pyramids were built around 1790 BC.

Valley of the Kings

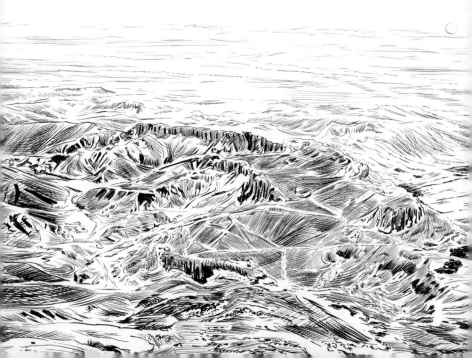

At the beginning
of the New Kingdom
(1550 BC), the pharaohs
again began to build
huge monuments to
themselves. These
were not pyramids,
however. They were
tombs carved out of
the rock cliffs in the
Valley of the Kings,
across the Nile from
Thebes. Along with them
were enormous temples,
like the one at Thebes
dedicated to the god
Amun-Re. It covers over
sixty-one acres. Ten of the
cathedrals of Europe could
fit inside it.

Amun-Re

The pharaoh Amenhotep III constructed two huge statues of himself in front of his tomb. Sixty feet high, these statues long puzzled archeologists. They appeared to be made from solid rock, but no one could understand how they were brought to the site. Then modern scientists discovered that the Egyptians of that time had made them out of stone slurry, a kind of clay that appears to be solid rock when dry.

Piye

Egypt had thrived under its pharaohs for thousands of years, but at last it began to weaken. The people high up the river, the Nubians (in present-day Sudan), had long been under Egyptian control. Around 750 BC, a Nubian warrior, Piye, brought his forces down the Nile. In only a year's time, the Nubians conquered Egypt. Piye was the first in a series of "black pharaohs"— dark-skinned Africans who ruled the country.

Piye and his descendants had great respect for Egyptian culture. They did not destroy the ancient monuments. Instead they copied Egyptian customs in their own land. Today there are more pyramids in Nubia than there are in Egypt.

A series of other conquerors ruled Egypt, and finally it became part of the Roman Empire. Egypt would not regain its independence until modern times.

Around 1600, European travelers and merchants began to bring home souvenirs of Egypt—small statues, jewelry, even mummies when they could be found. Europeans often ground up the mummies and used them as medicine.

In 1798, a new conqueror appeared on the horizon—Napoleon Bonaparte, future emperor of France. He brought scientists and artists along with his army. One of his artists later published a series of books showing the Great Pyramids and other wonders. They were best sellers all over Europe and set off a craze for Egyptian styles in furniture, pottery, and even architecture. An English poet wrote: "Everything must now be Egyptian; the ladies wear crocodile ornaments,

Napoleon Bonaparte

and one must sit on sphinxes in a room hung with mummies . . . who are enough to make children afraid to go to bed."

The world has never lost its interest in ancient Egypt. In 2010, more than fourteen million

tourists came to Egypt to see the pyramids and the Sphinx.

King Tut

The pharaohs of the Great Pyramids are not household names. The one pharaoh who most people know is King Tutankhamen. He is called King Tut for short. Yet Tut was a minor pharaoh who had a small four-room tomb. No pyramid. The reason he is so famous is that his tomb, which was discovered in 1922, had not been looted. It contained amazing treasures. Many are on display at the Cairo Museum.

The objects found in King Tut's tomb are too numerous to list. They included six chariots, many gold couches and beds, daggers and other weapons, thirty jars of wine, musical instruments, ostrich-feather fans, and many game boards made of ebony. Truly he was ready to have a good time in the afterlife. The golden mask that covered the young pharaoh's face weighed twenty-five pounds. That would make it worth half a million dollars today just for the gold. Since King Tut was only a minor pharaoh, we can only guess at the treasures that must have been buried with the three rulers in the Great Pyramids.

CHAPTER 7
Still Giving Up Their Secrets

Today, more than 4,500 years after the first pyramids were built, scientists are still discovering new secrets about them. In fact, in 2008, a pyramid was found that people had not even known existed. This was the tomb of Queen Sesheshet.

Her pyramid was five stories high and had been buried beneath the sand. Earlier archeologists had used the site as a dumping ground. It was the 118th pyramid to be discovered.

In 2013, archeologists discovered a surprising find at Tel Hazor, in Israel. It was a stone fragment showing the feet of a sphinx. Between the feet was carved the name of the pharaoh Menkaure, who built the third of the Great Pyramids. What was the sphinx doing there? Probably it was

brought to Tel Hazor by another people, the Hyksos, who conquered Egypt around 1650 BC. There may be more surprises as archeologists continue to explore Tel Hazor.

Even at Giza, where so much exploration has been done, there are recent finds. One of the most spectacular was made in 1954, right next to the Great Pyramid itself. Earlier archeologists had found that walls originally surrounded the pyramids. Now it was seen that one of these walls was closer than the others. The chief archeologist had it cleared away.

What he found was a large pit, covered up with giant stones sealed with plaster. Carefully, some of the plaster was chipped away. The chief archeologist was hit with a rush of hot air. "I closed my eyes," he wrote. "I smelled incense . . . I smelled time. . . . I smelled centuries." Inside the pit was an ancient boat. It had been hidden there for more than 4,500 years.

It took months of work to remove the stones (sixteen tons each) that covered the pit. The wooden boat was found to be in almost perfect condition. Except for one thing. The boat had been taken apart to fit into the pit. What the archeologists found was like a gigantic model kit. There were 1,224 pieces—and no instruction booklet! It took ten years to fit all the pieces of the boat together. Today, you can see it in a special museum at the foot of the Great Pyramid.

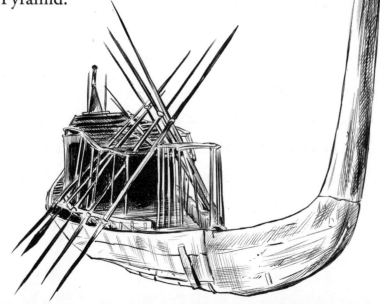

Since its discovery, people have wondered what the boat was used for. It was not just to carry the pharaoh on his journey to the afterlife. Markings show that the boat was actually used in real water. Perhaps it carried the pharaoh's body across the Nile to its final resting place.

Scientists have also come up with a new theory on how the Egyptians moved the massive stones for building the pyramids. Some people have suggested that the stones could have been placed on wooden sleds. But sleds with such heavy loads would sink in the desert sand around the pyramids. In 2014, researchers experimented with pouring water on the sand in front of sleds carrying heavy objects. The water made the sand hard and smooth. With enough people pulling the sled, it would move easily across the sand.

Proof for this idea came from a wall painting in the tomb of an important official of the Middle Kingdom. It shows 172 workers pulling a sled

holding a huge statue of the official. Sure enough, at the front of the sled is a man pouring water on the ground. Earlier researchers thought this was only a ceremony to make the ground pure. Now they realize it may have had a very practical purpose.

An even more interesting idea concerns the placement of the three Great Pyramids. At the time the pyramids were built, Egyptians had long observed the night skies. They knew of the constellation today called Orion. The Egyptians connected Orion with Osiris, god of rebirth and the afterlife. In the sky, Orion has three bright stars close together—called Orion's belt. The smallest of these three stars is placed at a slight angle from the other two.

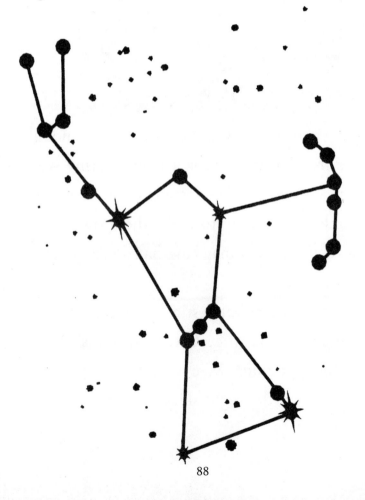

A researcher named Robert Bauval noticed that this is just the way the three Great Pyramids stand. The smallest of the three, built by Pharaoh Menkaure, is just off a straight line drawn through the other two. Bauval thinks this was on purpose. He says the Great Pyramids were intended to be an earthly mirror of Orion's belt.

Not all scientists agree with Bauval. Some point out that the angle of the stars is somewhat different from the angle of the pyramids. Others argue that the third star is north of the other two, while the smallest pyramid is south. What everybody agrees on is that we still do not know all the secrets of the pyramids.

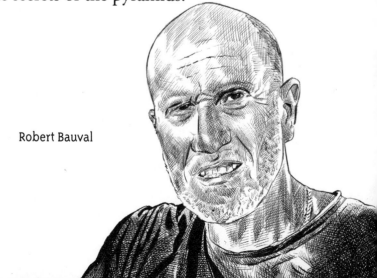

Robert Bauval

CHAPTER 8
Pyramids in Other Lands, Other Times

People in other places besides Egypt have built pyramids. There are many in Central America in the countries of Belize, El Salvador, Guatemala, and Honduras. Mexico has some spectacular pyramids. Those which were built from stone have staircases along one or more of their sides. These lead to a flattened area at the top, where temples were built out of wood. Religious ceremonies and sacrifices were carried out there.

At Tikal, in today's Guatemala, a roof comb stands on the top of the pyramid. This is a stone structure originally covered with plaster. Artists painted and carved pictures of gods and important rulers on the roof comb. (The comb part looks like the comb on a rooster's head.)

The earliest Central American pyramids were made of earth. One of the oldest is at La Venta. That's in the Mexican state of Tabasco. It was built by the Olmec people around 500 BC. Because it was made of earth, the sides have been eroded by rain. One or more Olmec leaders may have been buried inside, but no one knows for sure. There are no tunnels like the ones in the pyramids in Egypt.

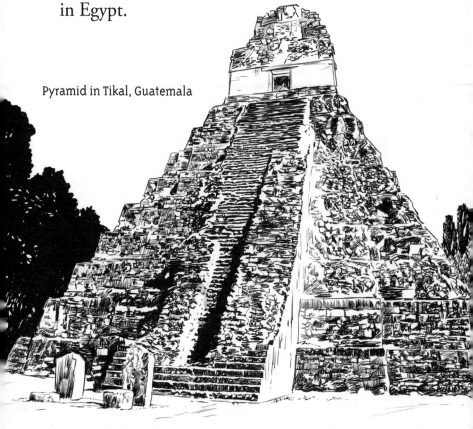

Pyramid in Tikal, Guatemala

The largest pyramid in Mexico is even bigger than the Great Pyramids in Egypt. It is known as the Great Pyramid of Cholula. It may have been dedicated to the Aztec serpent god. Made of stone, its base is three times the size of the base of the Great Pyramid at Giza. (But the one at Giza is taller.)

Great Pyramid of Cholula

Cholula was built in several stages over 1,200 years. Work began in the third century BC and continued on to the ninth century AD. Each time new building began, the workers covered up the older pyramid and built over it. The result is the largest monument ever made anywhere in the world.

About four hundred bodies have been discovered inside Cholula. But many of these were human sacrifices—not rulers. The bones of several children were found inside ceramic pots. The children were supposed to carry messages to the rain god, asking for dry weather to end.

Today, a Catholic church stands on top of the pyramid at Cholula. Because trees and grass have grown up along the sides, the pyramid appears to be a natural hill.

The third largest pyramid in the world is the Pyramid of the Sun near Mexico City. The Aztec people believed this was a holy spot where the gods who created the world had lived. Centuries after the pyramid was built, the city surrounding it was destroyed.

Even today, this pyramid remains a mysterious place. No one is sure what the people who built it called themselves. The pyramid was built between AD 100 and 250, and the city was burned around AD 650. Again, no one knows who destroyed it. Nearly all that was left were the Pyramid of the Sun and a smaller pyramid known as the Pyramid of the Moon.

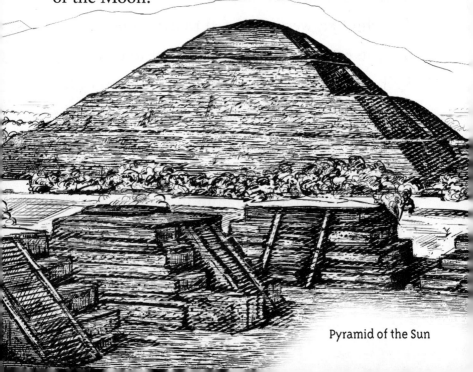

Pyramid of the Sun

Pyramid of the Magician

Near Uxmal, Mexico, is the Pyramid of the Magician. According to Mayan legend, there once was a boy who had been born from an egg. He was given a task by the local ruler. The boy had to build a pyramid in a single night, or he would be put to death. The boy had magic powers, and accomplished what seemed impossible. The pyramid was built overnight. What happened after that? The people overthrew their ruler and made the boy their king.

Pyramid of Tenayuca

The Pyramid of Tenayuca, also near Mexico City, is a double pyramid. Two pyramids were built next to each other and enlarged every fifty-two years from 1299 to 1507. Why was the number fifty-two important? The Mayan calendar lasted for fifty-two years, at the end of which everything had to be renewed.

One of the most popular tourist spots in Mexico is Chichen Itza, in the Yucatán Peninsula. The Maya people built a great city there around the tenth century AD. Many of its buildings still stand, including several pyramids. The largest of them is called El Castillo. It served as a temple to the feathered serpent god. El Castillo is a step pyramid with staircases up each of its four sides leading to a stone temple on top.

El Castillo

The people who built El Castillo had observed the movement of the sun. Each year, at the spring and autumn equinoxes (the two days in the year when day and night are of equal length), the pyramid displays an eerie signal. The steps on the northwest corner cast a shadow on the staircase of the north side. The shadow looks like a serpent wriggling down the stairs. Probably this was meant to be the serpent god.

There are countless pyramids in other parts of the world. Some, like the ones in Egypt, are in Africa. In Algeria, there is a pyramid-shaped tomb where a ruler was buried around 300 BC. And in Sudan, just south of Egypt, there are about 220 royal pyramids. They once held the bodies of the kings and queens of the Nubian Empire.

Quite a few granite pyramid-shaped temples were built in south India during the Chola dynasty (third century BC through the thirteenth century AD). Some of them are still in use today. One of them is said to be the first building ever built entirely of granite and finished within five years. In the Khmer Empire, in present-day Cambodia, pyramid-shaped temples were built around one thousand years ago.

Even the founders of the United States were

impressed by the pyramids. Look on the back of a dollar bill. There you will see the two sides of the Great Seal of the United States, designed in 1782. One of the sides shows a pyramid with an eye on top. The pyramid has thirteen layers of stones, for the original thirteen colonies. The eye represents an "all-seeing providence" that watches over the United States.

Forty-five centuries have gone by since the Great Pyramids were built. They are older than almost anything else constructed by humans. They have stood as dynasties rose and fell. They witnessed conquerors pass by over the centuries. They even resisted an attempt to destroy them. Six of the Seven Wonders of the Ancient World have vanished, mainly due to earthquakes and fires. But the Pyramids remain. Possibly they will still be standing as long as people live on the earth.

Modern Pyramids

People are still building pyramids. One of the most recent is the Luxor Hotel in Las Vegas, Nevada. With a surface wall of glass, it is 365 feet high—still not as tall as the Great Pyramids.

Luxor Hotel in
Las Vegas, Nevada

More Modern Pyramids

The Walter Pyramid, a sports arena in Long Beach, California, is eighteen stories high with aluminum sides. The famous Louvre Museum in Paris, France, has a pyramid-shaped glass entrance seventy feet high.

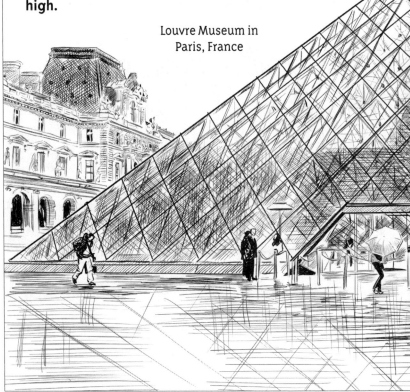

Louvre Museum in
Paris, France

The city of Memphis, Tennessee (named for the capital of ancient Egypt), has a basketball arena, thirty-two stories high, in the shape of a pyramid. Moody Gardens, a tourist attraction in Galveston, Texas, has three pyramids. One is an aquarium, one contains a rain forest, and the third, called the Discovery Pyramid, focuses on science exhibits.

Timeline of the Great Pyramids

c. 3100 BC	First pharaoh, Narmer, unites Upper and Lower Egypt
c. 2550 BC	Pyramid of Khufu (or Cheops) is built
c. 2520 BC	Pyramid of Khafre is built
c. 2500 BC	Great Sphinx is built
c. 2490 BC	Pyramid of Menkaure is built
c. 750 BC	Nubians from the south conquer Egypt
AD 1798	Napoleon Bonaparte brings scientists, artists, and his army to Egypt
1818	Italian collector Giovanni Belzoni discovers a small entrance to Khafre's pyramid
1903	William Flinders Petrie finds the only known image of Khufu at Abydos
1922	King Tut's tomb is discovered
2010	More than fourteen million tourists visit Egypt to see the Great Pyramids and the Sphinx

Timeline of the World

Due to climate change, the Sahara desert begins to spread in Africa	c. 3500 BC
Builders begin to erect Stonehenge in Wales	c. 2600 –2300 BC
The Bronze Age begins in Northern Europe	c. 2000 BC
King Solomon of Israel builds the first Temple of Jerusalem	c. 950 BC
Greek poet Homer writes *The Iliad*	c. 800 BC
Construction on the Great Wall of China begins	c. 221 BC
Cleopatra becomes queen of Egypt	51 BC
Construction of the Colosseum begins in Rome	c. AD 70
Italian astronomer Galileo discovers Jupiter's four largest moons	1610
The French Revolution begins	1789
World War I begins	1914
Liberia's Ellen Johnson Sirleaf becomes the first female leader in Africa in modern times	2006

Bibliography

*Books for young readers

El Mahdy, Christine. *The World of the Pharaohs*. New York: Thames and Hudson, 1987.

*Hart, George. *Ancient Egypt*. New York: DK, 2014.

Hellum, Jennifer. *The Pyramids.* Westport, CT: Greenwood Press, 2007.

*Henzel, Cynthia Kennedy. *Pyramids of Egypt*. Edina, MN: ABDO Publishing Co., 2011.

*Putnam, James. *Eyewitness: Pyramid*. New York: DK, 2004.

Schulz, Regine, and Matthias Seidel. *Egypt: The World of the Pharaohs*. Cologne, Germany: Konemann, 2004.

Verner, Miroslav. *The Pyramids: The Mystery, Culture, and Science of Egypt's Great Monuments*. New York: Grove Press, 2001.

Williams, A.R. "Egypt's Animal Mummies," *National Geographic*, November 2009, 30–57.

ALEXANDRIA

NILE RIVER
DELTA

GIZA

RED
PYRAMID

BENT
PYRAMID

NILE RIVER